So

Take Time

Text and Illustrations by Mike Artell

Dominie Press, Inc.

Publisher: Raymond Yuen
Series Editor: Stanley L. Swartz
Consultant: Adria F. Klein
Editor: Bob Rowland
Designers: Lois Stanfield and Debra Dickerson
Illustrator: Mike Artell

Published by:

ᴨᶜᶩ Dominie Press, Inc.

1949 Kellogg Avenue
Carlsbad, California 92008 USA

www.dominie.com

ISBN 0-7685-0729-4

Printed in Singapore by PH Productions Pte Ltd
1 2 3 4 5 6 PH 03 02 01

ITP

Some things happen right away.
Others take some time.
If you help me, we can read
about them in this rhyme.

Some things happen right away,
like turning on a light.

Some things take a little time,
like the sunrise that's so bright.

Some things happen right away,
like watching TV shows.

Some things take a little time,
like reading when it snows.

Some things happen right away,
like food that's on the shelf.

Some things take a little time,
like growing food yourself.

Some things happen right away,
like running fast in races.

Some things take a little time,
like tying your shoelaces.

Some things happen right away,
like games you like to play.

Some things take a little time,
like putting games away.

Some things happen right away, like making a mistake.

Some things take a little time,
like fixing what you break.

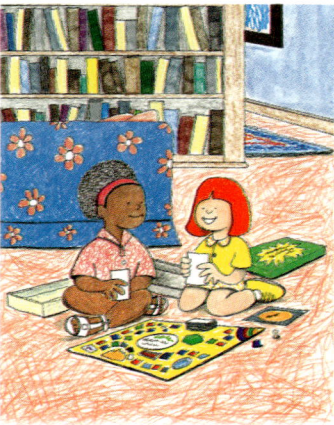
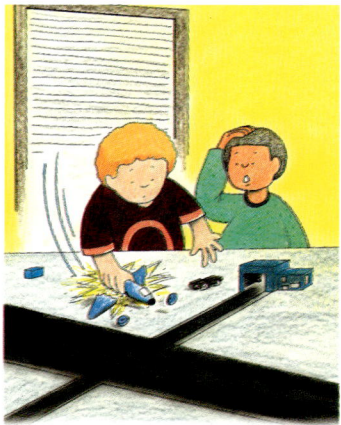

Some things happen right away,
and they are lots of fun.
It's nice when you don't have to wait
for something to be done.

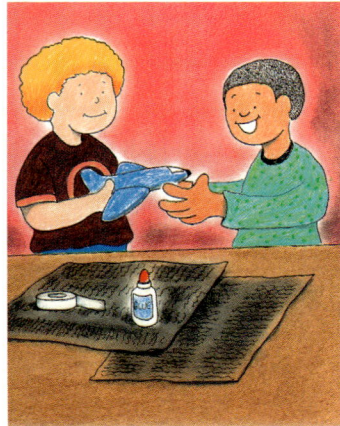

But some things take a little time,
and though it's hard to wait,
if everything did happen fast,
we might miss something great.